Sit, Mits!

By Debbie Croft

It is Tim.

It is Mits.

Mits!

Mits is at the pit.

Mits sat at the tap and ...

Tim sat at the pit!

Mits! Sit and sip.

CHECKING FOR MEANING

1. Where does Mits want to go? *(Literal)*

2. How does Tim try to stop Mits? *(Literal)*

3. Why did Tim sit at the pit? *(Inferential)*

EXTENDING VOCABULARY

Mits	How many sounds are in the word *Mits*? What other words do you know that begin with the same sound as *Mits*?
pit	Look at the word *pit*. What does the word *pit* mean in this story? What else can it mean?
at	Look at the word *at*. Find two words in the story that rhyme with *at*. What other words can you think of that rhyme with these words?

MOVING BEYOND THE TEXT

1. What does Tim do in the story to try to take care of Mits? What else do you need to do to take care of a dog?

2. Where do you think Tim and Mits went after the end of the story?

3. Do you like to play in puddles? Why or why not?

4. What can you do outside during wet weather?

SPEED SOUNDS

Mm	Ss	Aa	Pp	Ii	Tt

PRACTICE WORDS

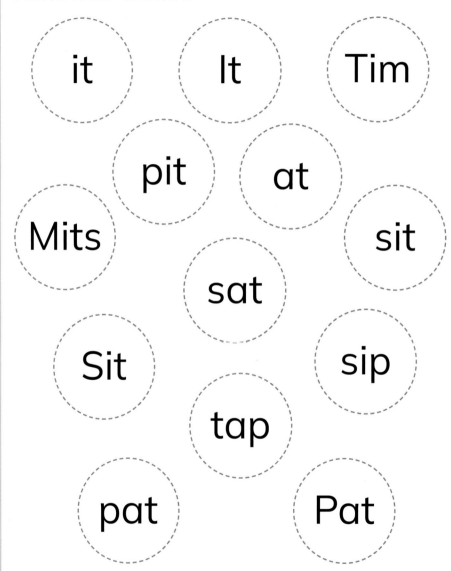

it

It

Tim

pit

at

Mits

sit

sat

Sit

sip

tap

pat

Pat